M000208291

even now

jill sabella & rosemerry wahtola trommer

Even Now
Copyright © 2016 by Jill Sabella
& Rosemerry Wahtola Trommer

Design & layout by Kyle Harvey
Cover Image by Jill Sabella

Even Now
Jill Sabella & Rosemerry Wahtola Trommer
ISBN 978-0-9962170-9-5
Lithic Press

LITHIC PRESS
fine books for an old planet

www.lithicpress.com

for our young ones, Steele, Finn, Vivian and Shawnee

Introduction

As every artist knows, something magic can happen with collaboration—it becomes a glorious illogical equation in which one plus one equals much more than we might expect. It doesn't always work this way, but when it does, oh!

In the summer of 2014, we met via email. We'd both been invited to participate in a collaborative show, 12 x 2, curated by Jill Scher, to be hosted at the Art Center in Carbondale. Though we were strangers, we quickly discovered a common appreciation for simplicity—a leaning toward less and the more that blossoms out of it.

And so came the concept of three lines. For over a year, we devoted ourselves to exploring collaborative threes in poetry and visual art. Half of the pieces began with three-line poems that inspired three-line images. Then we played with having the images come first with poems emerging from the art.

We were surprised, delighted and humbled by these intimate, creative heart-to-hearts. And we were thrilled to learn how much others enjoyed them, too, when we finally shared them in the summer of 2015. The original 12 poems were done with a letterpress on rice paper and paired with brush drawings done in Sumi ink on rice paper. These were placed in three 4-foot-long, horizontal frames with four "conversations" each. All three of these pieces sold on opening night.

Though the show was over, we knew our exploration was just beginning, and we spent the next year creating a total of 45 pairings.

This book you are holding is in some ways the culmination of the project, but what you will perhaps see or feel as you turn the pages is that something much more than a book evolved out of this process—a deep friendship. A willingness for two hearts to open more than they thought they could so that they might meet each other in new and unpredictable ways.

We hope you enjoy this additional journey into three, in which the poem is one piece, and the image is another, and you, dear readers, are the third.

—Rosemerry Wahtola Trommer and Jill Sabella

undoing another button

given wings

unruly blossoms

even
now

my heart an apple blossom
afraid it doesn't know
how to become an apple

standing at the edge
the first step
is the only step

this terrible ache–
giving it the best seat
at my table

sunset so pink
the mind undoes another button—
the whole world blushes

here, I'm thirsty
said my cheek
to your tear

losing all my petals
I did not yet know I would
lose my stem, too

even now, even now,
even now, even now, even now,
even now, bow

I throw my hunger
into the river, then, too alone,
jump in after it

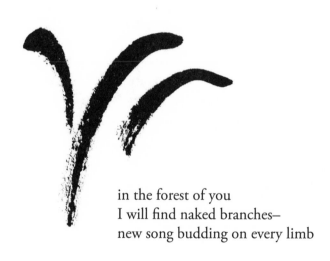

in the forest of you
I will find naked branches–
new song budding on every limb

this wound—
re-teaching my tongue to name it
blessing

empty pockets—
this, too,
is a gift

slipping this love letter
under the narrow gap
of the wrong door

still unfurling into bloom,
this flower I thought
was fully opened

the house on fire
and me still trying
to get all the beds made

walking miles for a drink
not noticing in the back yard
a well

it's not what I
expected said the fish
given wings

every inch of me parched
still these lips
too shy to ask for rain

is it one small child
or the whole world
I cradle

wondering why
the candle doesn't give light
never offering it flame

that loud crow—
trying to quiet the part of me
that wants it to be quiet

blowing all the wishes
off the dandelion—
falling in love with nothing

waiting for forgiveness—
the train is ready
but the rails long gone

after swallowing the sea
still thirsting
for a lake

this old idea
I slip into again—
a silk dress lined with glue

the same rich tea—
drinking it from different cups
together

in the river of self
surprised to find I am also
the dam, the eddy

even sad songs
are good for dancing–
moonlight in an empty hand

two hands holding
a vase, even the loveliest vase,
can't open a door

an ant never
walks backward—
learning to love like that

twelve-armed love—
two arms to hold you
ten to let you go

before the dawn
the possibility of dawn—
all night holding that

the next true thing—
a wind that begins far away
unbraids my hair

steep, this trail—
one more reason to stop often
and notice how beautiful

but it was written
in stone, said the woman
to the sand

in a quiet room
the sound of footseps
years ago

regardless where I stand
I never see all of you—
oh, unruly blossoms

scent of spring—
even the shadows
grow buds

all day
tugging on my sleeve—
this kiss

standing
on my own welcome mat
roses in hand

that fence I build
around my heart—
real good kindling

shoveling
the walk, making a path
for the sun

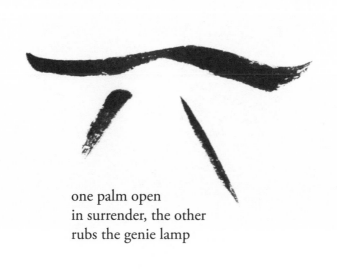

one palm open
in surrender, the other
rubs the genie lamp

just when the bonfire
burns beyond control
throwing in another stick

not knowing
how to pray, I learn to practice
astonishment

you and I—
two threads joined in one
miraculous cloth

Jill Sabella has been involved in the visual arts all her life, finding expression through handcolored photography, drawing, painting and sculpture. She lives in Old Snowmass, Colorado.

This body of work with Rosemerry was the beginning of a new form of visual expression—which came with a brush, sumi ink and rice paper—as a call for or a response to a "haikuling" of Rosemerry's. The magical interface of her words and my images took us both by surprise and amazement.

Rosemerry Wahtola Trommer's poetry has appeared in *O Magazine*, in back alleys, on *A Prairie Home Companion* and on river rocks. She was appointed Poet Laureate of Colorado's Western Slope (2015-2017) and co-directs the Talking Gourds Poetry Club. Since 2006, she's written a poem a day. Favorite one-word mantra: *Adjust*.

Her launch into three-line poems was first inspired by her dear friend and mentor James Tipton, and the collaboration with Jill transformed her understanding of what three lines and two hearts can do.